Life
Love
and a
Legacy of Poetry

John Howard

Husky Trail Press LLC

Contact the author at:
John Howard
C/O Jean McQuade
PO Box 87
Rockville, RI 02873

ISBN 978-1-935258-21-6

Husky Trail Press LLC
PO Box 705
East Lyme, CT 06333
www.huskytrailpress.com
info@huskytrailpress.com

Dedication

To my wife and family

Acknowledgments

My most humble and sincere thanks to my daughter Jean (Howard) McQuade for grabbing the bull by the horns and pushing for this publication. Many thanks to Lisa (Howard) Vuono for the peace and tranquility of her home and gardens within which some of my poetry could germinate. For my daughter Joyce Howard, I cannot say enough about her prodding and pushing for me to publish. The rolling hills and pristine horse farms of Virginia outlined by the Appalachian Mountains provided an excellent potential for the writing of poetry. For this I give thanks to my daughter Karen (Howard) Mitchell. For missions of finding "the right" photograph, many thanks to Michela (McQuade) Champlin, Jean McQuade, Joyce Howard, and Marikate Lynch. The cover design is the product of Joyce Howard…Thanks. To Janice Higgins-Rissler for her help. My special thanks to Sheila Murphy Adams who did the typing, editing, chasing down publishers, and many other tasks required for the completion of this book. Last, but not least, to Ralphina, I give my love and many thanks for putting up with my quirks and questions in the writing of this book.

Contents

Summer Night Walk on the Beach

To walk on the beach on a warm summer night
The waves accented with the moon's eerie light

A soft balmy breeze caresses your face
The blessing of being in such a marvelous place

The splendor of nature in all of its glory
It is amazing to me as it weaves out its story

There is nothing but water as far as you see
With the pounding of the surf as it reaches out to me

My bare feet in the sand stirring phosphorous grains as I stroll
Like fireflies converging on a small grassy knoll

The pull of the water as it withdraws from the shore
Sifting the sand through my toes, filling my tracks ever more

Seaweed on the shore takes on images in the shimmering light
Causing imagination to wander as it doesn't look quite right

There are views from a distance that cause all the wonder
You walk closer to the images and discover your blunder

John Howard

That it is just that old seaweed on the shore in the night
Giving off reflections in the soft moon light

A boat on the distant horizon so far
With the light in the cabin twinkling soft, like a star

To stand out in the water and gaze out in awe
And wonder at their travels - whoever they are

This is a night to forget all your troubles and cares
For imagination to wander at new thoughts and new dares

To reflect on your course as you pass along life's way
And give thanks to the Lord for another great day

July 28, 1993

Reflections—Yawgoog Road

A look at some land alongside a lake
Overgrown with weeds with a house in sad shape
Old wrecks in the yard with cats running 'round
A barn full of junk overflowing its bounds.

The house on the land was a cape of small size
Only "loving care needed" in the Realtor's eyes…

Still, all in all, without all the glamour
We should envision some beauty mixed into the pallor
Of faded out siding and overgrown trees
Rusted screen doors, broken windows, giving home to some bees.

By cleaning the yard and changing the structure
Of stripping the house back to the original luster

Just maybe we could find what we knew would be there
A charming old house with its own private flair.

A bargain was struck and an offer was tended
Now all that was needed was the deal not amended.

It all came about very quickly for sure…
The property was ours, now we felt quite secure.

The original plans for the lay of the land
After cleaning and clearing got a bit out of hand.

The home got chopped up with a lot of elation…
It was picked up and moved to another location.

An addition was added just as large as the cape
Post and Beam construction outlined its shape.

It all came together, dowels and pegs in their place
Large beams and small beams outlining the space.

A colonial look is what appeared from the front view
Yet contemporary structure graced the rear that was new.

The house was positioned to follow the sun and to pick up its rays...
With large vented windows for both beauty and warmth on cold
    winter days.

An alcove projected out exterior from one wall
As a small breakfast nook set aside from it all.
Surrounded by glass, yet cozy to feel,
Made eating with nature a part of the meal.

A deck was applied to the rear, wrapped around
The house, on the south side, where the view did abound.

The lake in its splendor did enhance the scene
Looking over the trees, the house did careen.

To sit on the lake, in a boat, looking back
Toward the house that used to look like a shack.

Recalling the work and the thoughts, the duress
The many long hours, the decisions and stress...

The shape of the house gardens worked to create
A beach and a raft floating soft on the lake.

All of these things that fill you with pride
Make you feel good, with nothing to hide.

Don't think of this place of just wood and stone...
Look at it lovingly and then
Call it home.

August 5, 1993

before

after

Contemplation of Spring

A walk in the park with a comely young lass
The fresh smell of dew on the sprouting new grass
Hand in hand as you walk, your face in the sun
The warmth of the day makes adrenaline run.

The wonder unfolds as we pause to observe
That winter has left, with its drab reserves
Making way for the blossoms of spring to behold
The deep greens of leaves and bright flowers so bold.

Oh how I wonder just where I fit in
How the Lord has prepared me and how to begin
To expound all the virtues of life in the spring
As the beauty of nature makes my heart start to sing.

In this day and age as my body grows old
I think of my youth when I was so bold
With no time to spare to get where I was going
Just planning ahead but not ever knowing
What life was about in this hectic time
With no moment to spare, no reason or rhyme.

The vision of life is not hard to find
If you only pause and take out some time
Just put it aside, find some quiet place
Get out of the mainstream, step out of the race.

John Howard

On a balmy spring day, in an out of the way place, with no strife
This is the way to focus in on your life
To sit in the shade, and just contemplate
Take plenty of time, it pays off to wait
Bask in nature's splendor and think as dreamers will do
If you wait long enough, your dreams will come true.

June 1993

Earl

He's out bright and early at the start of the day
Observing different things that he passes on his way.

To wherever he's going, destination unknown
He calls it his office, his natural home.

It may be for coffee at a small sandwich shop
Head off to the library or to his bench in the park.

To whomever he meets as he hurries along
There's always a greeting like a verse of a poem.

We know not what he thinks as he passes us by
For his mind always wanders, his thoughts go awry.

He notices objects and envisions what we cannot see
Like the form of a woman in the bark of a tree.

The dew on a flower in the morning's bright light
Reflecting the sun like a star late at night
As it twinkles with color as the drops start to run
Like a prism catches light, it reflects from the sun.

He's observant of things, sometimes weird and eccentric
Not always straight lines, direct or concentric

Looking for holes, where holes shouldn't be
He sure doesn't act like you or like me.

He is very well read, perhaps to a fault
Maybe self-education trapped him in his vault.

Where, at times, his intelligence is accompanied by fact
The deductions of reason are jaded and cracked.

With the only one understanding his pleas of warning, of disaster
Is his own delusions of what's happening hereafter.

The answer to it all, comes as an obvious elation...
Take notice of Earl, for he's off medication.

April 10, 1994

Déjà Vu

I alighted from the bus in this quaint little town
Just passing on thru as I traveled around.

Wondering why I had decided to get off at this stop
For there was no one about, not even a cop.

As I walked down the street toward the center of town
I started to notice small things while I looked around.

It was like I was revisiting a place from my past
But where, or when, I knew this couldn't last.

For I had never been here before in my life
Nor seen any pictures or dreamed it so nice.

Yet as I progressed further into it all
I knew where I was going, each structure, each wall.

The place I was seeking now came into view
A decrepit old house, this was it, I just knew.

A little old woman sat across from the gate
She must have been ninety, to estimate her date.

The place was abandoned after the owner had died
But the taxes were paid from some funds put aside.

The owner was a lady, said the old woman, with a sigh
I blurted out "Molly," not knowing just why.

John Howard

"Molly" was correct, as the owner, she said
But for sixty some years she now had been dead.

She spoke to me, in a simple and matter-of-fact tone
Of an unwed young lady, dying at childbirth, alone.

Waiting for her long lost love to return
Who had left for the gold fields, his fortune to earn.

He returned the year after, not knowing her fate
He had brought fame and fortune, too little, too late.

They found him next morning out in back, near the sea
He had hung himself on the limb of a tree.

This all had transpired some sixty years back
Long before I arrived on this earth to keep track.

I wondered, out loud, how I knew of this lore
For I was quite sure I have not been here before

How could I explain just how that I knew,
The only recourse is it's just déjà vu.

May 5, 1994

What If

What if you knew when you were young what you know now
And you didn't have to live by the sweat of your brow.

What if children grew up with no worries or cares
And you didn't get breathless when climbing up stairs.

What if chores that you do didn't tire you at all
And you didn't get chilly in the winter or late fall.

What if luck always was with you so you didn't have to dare
And as you grew older, you still had your hair.

What if you always felt cheerful with no malice at all
With never a let down and never a fall.

What if people were loving and friendly each day
And they were ever so caring in the things that they say.

What if you could always feel the warmth of the sun and its rays
As you plod thru life on those long, dreary days.

What if all of these things should suddenly appear to be real
As you look at yourself and the way that you feel.

When you have struggled thru life in all of its states
Then you have passed thru it all to those heavenly gates.

August 1993

A Poet

A poet is a person who is difficult to describe
Who writes down thoughts in rhythm or rhyme

Who has visions or dreams of places or things
Then writes down on paper whatever it brings

There is no simple reason to describe how it's done
For poetry rolls out like the beats on a drum

It is truly amazing to review what you've written
Then to analyze the text and see how you're smitten

The writer will pause in the day to observe a spider in his play
Of spinning a web in just such a way to catch the glimmer of a sunny ray

To stop, to listen to the warbler's song
As it flits from branch to branch
Stopping only so long
As to give off his message of melodious cheer
For those who are willing to lend of an ear.

The cast of a shadow of an old mighty oak
Gives off an image on the soft grassy slope
That lengthens with time as the sun moves away
To encompass the landscape with its dark greens and grey.

The blaze of the flowers as they bloom in the spring
The rustling of leaves as they move with the wind.

The laughter of children at play in the park
The glare of a lamppost as it pushes out at the dark.
Silhouettes on the water backed up by the moon
The smell of mowed grass on an evening in June.

All these scenes and more cause the poet to pause
As he ponders his thoughts and looks for a cause
To pick up a pencil to jot down a phrase or a note
For the words of a poem will burst forth to be wrote.

We'll never know why, or when, or where
Wherever we are or whatever we've done
To look and observe what we see going on
To describe it in words of verse or of song.

The ways of a poet cannot be explained
For words come from the heart that cannot be contained
They bubble right out of the tip of the pen
We put those words away and start all over again.

It must be magic or so it must seem
As we while away time putting together the scheme
Of how it will sound as we read it out loud
Will it be harsh and brassy? or will it be soft, like a cloud?

Whatever it sounds like as it comes about
Are only my feelings as I phrase it all out.

Some will laugh at this poem while others will love it
For it's not only just words,
It's the work of a poet.

May 15, 1994

Summer Concert in the Park

They have planned and rehearsed with the music and song
To perform it just right when this night comes along.

For the people of the town in this great endeavor
Have worked oh so hard to put it together.

It's only one night of three hundred and sixty five
When the juices will flow to make it come alive.

The air is electric as we take in the view
Of the vendors, the ushers, performers, and crew.

Not to leave out the people, who are milling about
Talking to friends and to neighbors or just plain laying out
On their blankets enjoying the warm summer air
On this evening in June, in the park with grass mowed with care.

The sweet smell of roses hangs light in the soft evening breeze
When our blanket is spread in the shade of some large maple trees.

Picnic baskets are open with good food and drink galore
On a night like tonight who could ask for anything more.

Morris Men dancing in old English costumes, hand made
Waling sticks clacking in time with the concertinas serenade.

The shrill of a tin whistle helps to liven the beat
As the dancers mark time with their quick stomping feet.
The families are gathered on the blankets set out on the ground
Early in the dark to mark off their special compound.
Balloons have been bought and tied out on a line
Stretched out in the sky in an arc they're defined.

John Howard

Dusk now approaches and it's time to direct our attention
To the major festivities and to observe the perfection
Of a chorus that numbers more than a hundred voices strong
Yet defines quite so clearly the words of each song.

The orchestra plays and the crowd quiets down
As the music inspires, beguiles, and surrounds
The valley, the hills, the leaves and the trees...
Just look at the children, how they're all now at ease.
The cannons are ready as we all sit and wait
As the 1812 Overture starts to abate.

It's the close of the evening, twilight has settled to dark
The crowd has grown quieter this night in the park.

The cannons have blasted in time with the song
The Carrolons of Christ Church, in the distance, chime along.

At last, the finale has started, what we are here for and why
The roar and the flash of the fireworks
As they burst and lite up the sky

The orchestra plays, the chorus sings on in an exuberant manner
As the flag now unfurls from the podium to the words of the Star
Spangled Banner.

The fireworks now climax as they pull out all the stops
It's another great show for the "Westerly Summer Pops."

July 1994

23

Thoughts of a Soldier On the Line

Alone in this strange land halfway around mother earth
In the uniform of your country, fighting for this land, for whatever
    it's worth.

Wondering about the sacrifice of all those people in this time of strife
What's it all about... Is it all worth it... This fighting and this loss of
    life?

No one has clearly defined the issue, it's politics all the way
That has lead to this confusion, to this conflict we're in today.

We are out here in the trenches, fearing each day we're alive
That today won't be that day of days chalked up for me to die.

The weather is hot and humid with not a breath of air
My clothes are sticking to me, the dirt and sweat has matted my hair

I cleaned my rifle good last night, oiled it with loving care
Let's pray it remains quiet tonight, so I won't have to test it
Firing at shapes and forms everywhere

My girl's picture is in my helmet liner
That's what I should be thinking about and how
I should take off my old steel helmet, look at the picture
Cause I cannot envision what she looks like right now.

But I know if I take off that helmet,
Sure as there is a moon in the sky
A stray bullet from someone will find me,
And today is the day I will die.

John Howard

Hunker down in the dirt, forget all that stuff
About dying and killing and such
Make yourself smaller, get closer to the ground,
Hope that the earth will cover you up.

Pray that nothing bad will happen,
It's been a bright and peaceful day
Let no thoughts interrupt this spell
Keep on going, keep plodding away.

Keep your senses alert, don't waver
I wonder who's making those sounds?
Let's hope it's one of our guys
Checking up, or making the rounds.

A flare just went up, on my left,
Lighting up the area from out of the sky
Another one popped, I think I see something
I'm not sure, hold your fire, let the darkness adjust to your eye.

Almost morning now, light beginning to outline the hill
No events to report, no action, the landscape is quiet and still.

Morning is always the best part of the day
The birds are awake and starting their chatter
I wonder what event will occur on its way
To change my life...
          Oh! It just doesn't matter.

For I'm stuck in this place for the rest of the week
Two days to go before we get relief
Then it's time to get ready for me to go home
My turn is over; no longer reason to complain of my grief.

Crawl out of my hole in the dawn's chilly light
Stretch and shake out the cramps of the night
Watch out where you walk, for there might be a mine.
What's that loud noise?
        Bright light?
                Oh God, it's my time!

July 1994
Reflections of Korea - 1953

Naples, Florida

A balmy breeze, over a pure white beach,
caresses the shore
With rippling waves rebounding, exposing shells,
more and more.

The palm trees swaying in rhythm,
Smoothing the picture of gentle sea and soft balmy air
To expose nature's blend of a delicate lifestyle,
so warm and so fair.

The shells exposed by the water's wrath
Tell tales of storms and creatures past
That buried the shells we now exhort
Where did they exist in their life, so short?

The walk by the shore in the warmth of the day
Observing the children, in the sand, as they play,
To lie in the water, refreshingly soft
Looking into puffy white clouds, billowing high aloft.

The flight of the pelican, hovering over the bay,
Searching for food, eyeing the water for prey.
Ignoring the people, the boats, structures and docks
Only looking for fish in this strange paradox.

High-rise buildings abound up north on the shore
Strange in their contrast to the natural décor
One only must ponder, who was the teacher of this class
Who tried to outdo nature with concrete and glass.

John Howard

I've walked many beaches, long hours at a time
Observing and thinking, while feeling so fine.
Hand in hand with my lady in a romantic way
I haven't found anywhere better to stay.

To extol all the virtues of this nice southern place
Would take too much time, in this limited space.
When I sit back and think of this place, when alone
I hear distant voices, Naples is calling...
Calling me home!

January 1994

To Our Children, with Love

A little explanation from your mother and me
To try to sort out things about what we've tried to be
In raising our children in our simple manner
To help you and guide you without any glamour.

We know we're not perfect
Nor did we pretend to be
We're just plain Mom and Dad,
Your wonderful mother and me.

We tried to be role models, in each and every way
So that as you grew up, what you observed each day
Were parents you looked up to for guidance and care
Not fair weather parents who just happened to be there.

We tried to be someone you could talk with
When the going seemed to get tough
Who could answer most of your questions
And guide you through the rough.

Who you could turn to and depend on
when help was to be realized
Not get evasive answers,
or at best, be criticized.

We tried to be thoughtful and caring
As events pertained to you
Not put you back in second place
When it interfered with what we wanted to do.

John Howard

Sometimes we had to say "No" to a seemingly urgent request
Not in trying to hurt you, it's just what we thought best
For it's love that guides us in all of our ways
To help you to cope, to get through those tough and torturous days.

Give us your love, for that says it best
It will guide us and help us as we take our rest
From raising our children, our work and our stress
To take time to reflect on our children
Now that they are gone and have flown from our nest.

July 1994

Dreams of the Battlefield

In my vision I have seen death riding on a tremendous jet-black
    cloud.
Unleash his sword of lightening, striking bolts against the ground.
The stench of smoldering ashes make my nostrils flare.
As the lightening bolts with claps of thunder permeate the air.

The smell of sulfur and of powder combined with burning flesh.
Tears my eyes and dulls my mind with this unholy mess.

I can't believe what I've just witnessed, unfold before my eyes.
It's over as soon as it started I suddenly realize.
I'll push it back within my thoughts, this carnage I behold.
Back in the darkest corner, beyond retrieval, never to be told.

But thru the years, as I've grown old, the memory never dulls.
It pops up within my dreams, late at night, with all the thrills.
To toss and turn, relive this thing that eats away my brain.
Cold sweats, stiffened joints in the morning, my body feeling drained.

It's something I must carry,
This cross that I must bear.
This guilt or shame I'm feeling,
Just for being there.

Oh well, it's over now, at least that's the way it seems.
I wonder when this will come again, this crazy life-like dream?

John Howard

My guess is that it will never end.
I'm a witness to this game.
That grown men play with relish,
And call it "WAR" by name.

I never was the warrior type,
Soldiering's not for me.
Maybe this dream is my reminder—
To be the best that I can be.
Not to lose my temper,
To walk away from strife
To gently stroll thru everyday
And try to live a happy life.

September 1994

33

Autumn Morning

Awake, my soul, for night is done.
Come bask in the warmth of this glorious sun.
The mist softly rising thru the majestic oak trees
Piercing the forest with the light beams that it cleaves.

The rapture of the silence that surrounds this scene
Brings peace and contentment to this body, it seems.
As we partake of the beauty of the forest and glen
In our solitude, waiting for the day to begin.

The dew that has settled on the Maple's leaves
Glistens in the web that the tiny spider weaves.
The peace, the silence, astounds the senses
The intruder, called man, insignificant with his presence.

The blaze of color this autumn morn
Fulfills the promise of why we were born.
The beauty of nature around us abounds.
Behold, take stock, as you wander around.

The gift of the creator in osmosis prevails
Scarlets, bright yellows on hills, with green in the valleys
Where frost has not touched the leaves with its magic
Awaits its turn as the brush from the pallet.

John Howard

Sure in your knowledge that summer is done
The cool morning air, a premonition of winter to come.
Squirrels are busy storing acorns and nuts
Stopping only so long to listen and look.

This scene that we witness, this treasure we observe
Is ever so fleeting, take the time you deserve
To reflect on your being and why you are here
Get closer to nature...
The answer is clear.

October 9th 1994
A Beautiful Day!

Dreams

What is it that you do in the middle of the night?
As you lay in your bed and turn out the light
When your mind takes over and closes your eyes
Imagination runs wild, visions start to arrive.

It all seems so real, are you asleep or awake?
Is it part of a dream that your mind tries to create?
It's vivid, intense, almost real so it seems.
Am I living this truly or is it just part of my dream?

Reality is nothing, my mind works it out.
I can hear every sound, yet no one's about.
It's totally clear, these words that I shout.
I open my mouth and no sound comes out.

I can run, I can leap, I can roll down a hill.
Yet my body is inert, I lay perfectly still.
My emotions run rampant, I laugh or I cry.
Sometimes I sit up, but I never know why.

The people I meet are indelibly clear,
Yet they utter no sound that I can hear.
They may have a message for me to retain.
My mind does not receive it, not by sound, this refrain.

It is amazing to me how this all comes about
Sometimes I remember, my mind culls it out
More often it's gone with the light of the day
Another night's dream has just faded away.

November 30, 1994

John Howard

Enders Island

It's a small jewel of an island,
Off the Connecticut shore, in the Long Island Sound.
Connected to the mainland via a causeway
Where the salt air is pungent, sea creatures abound.
The Edmundite Fathers caretake this quiet, peaceful,
Out of the way place.
Where they invite many faithful to come, to contemplate,
And to partake of God's Grace.

The peace is enveloping,
It surrounds and inspires with its pull.
Natural background noises, waves lapping,
The occasional shrill cry of a gull.
To serenely gaze upon the restless water
Slapping listlessly against this small piece of land.
To silently contemplate the fragile daffodil
That I now hold within my hand.

The feeling of contentment as one withdraws unto one's self.
Contemplation is now king, the feeling purely is Top Shelf.
As we focus within our mind, concentrate where we are.
Dimensions of our space are near, not very far.

The oneness of ourself, as we dwell
On this ever smaller, precious earth
Makes us analyze our self, our needs, our deeds,
What we've accomplished and what we're worth.

John Howard

To get closer to our maker is what it's all about
To reflect upon our past, ask forgiveness, get it out.
Cleanse out the system, confession, it's true
Bring it to the surface, it's definitely good for you.

You're alone, by yourself, only answer to the Lord—he's your tool.
No reason to lie or cheat, for there is no one here to fool.
Test only yourself; use your mind as your foil.
Ask for grace and forgiveness; use this island for your toil.

Use prayer as your vehicle, go one on one with the Lord
Bare your soul, get it out, only you know the reason why
It's just between you and your God, this Island and the sky.

April 23, 1995

What Do You See?

What do you see out the window today?
The sun is out bright, it's springtime, a young farmer cutting hay.
A small youth follows, running, jumping with glee.
I stare at that lad, for I'm looking at me.

What do you see out the window today?
A youth, sowing seed, in a field newly plowed.
A man and a woman watching over, so proud.
A middle-aged couple watching their son at his toil.
I know the feelings of that boy, as he works with the soil.

What do you see out the window today?
A grown man, in a uniform, is coming up the road.
He walks with assurance, proud, strong, easily shouldering his load.
I recognize that fellow, as I gaze from afar.
It's me, coming home from a long forgotten war.

What do you see out the window today?
A happy young couple, he with a small child on his knee.
And she, pushing another on a swing, attached to a tree.
A feeling of contentment, of warmth, and of love, fills the air.
It's the prime of my life that I'm witnessing out there.

John Howard

What do you see out the window today?
An elderly couple, grandchildren in tow.
As they go down a road that once was a field, new houses in a row.
Everyone's in a hurry on these brisk autumn days,
　　　No smiles, no laughter,
Whatever happened to our leisurely ways?

What do you see out the window today?
I can't see a thing, the window glazed over with snow.
It's got to be the future that I'm looking for, I know.
There's only just dreariness and darkness on this dark winter day.
But I know there's a light out there somewhere to show me the way.

October 28, 1996

Imagination

Now winter is upon us, the weather is strictly a bore.
These dreary, drab days, cold wind driving snow in off the shore.
I sit and I stare, my mind off into space,
Trying to imagine myself away from this dreadful place.

I think of warm breezes, palms swaying, pelicans diving for fish.
Of warm sand, being barefoot, bright sun is my wish.
Going fishing, rocking gently in clear water near a cay
But I'm only day dreaming, this is the bright spot of my day.

Imagination: I'm told is a wonderful tool we must sharpen and hone.
To be used by us all when we are feeling blue and alone.
We must put it to use in our own special way.
To overcome those "blah's," to get on with our day.

Shift your mind into gear, form a picture on your mental screen.
Think only good thoughts, get into your dream.
Make it Technicolor, make it vivid, clear the details in your mind.
On with the program, treat this vision as prime time.

When you're awakened, quite abruptly, your attention now caught
Remember to file away your vision, for it's not all for naught.
Instant recall is with me, I just have to remember the way
Then I can bring it all back again on my next dreary day.

December 3, 1996

John Howard

Prelude to **Uncle Nickie's Wine**

Every Italian family has someone… an Uncle Nicky out there in the family. A person who stands out, who really enjoys a lusty meal, good company… a rousing discussion with his companions over a hearty glass of homemade wine. This is the person who enjoys his garden, his home, making homemade supra, rich crusty Italian bread, and most of all… the company of family and friends. When your thoughts drift his way it makes your taste buds tingle, your heart fill with warmth and your head fill with fond memories, then to that person, the poem is dedicated.

"Uncle Nickie's Wine"

by John Howard Steffan

Let me pass along to you a little story concerning our kin and kind.
Of the good times, the warmth, the memories, and Uncle Nickie's wine.

I don't know where the grapes are grown nor do I know who tends the vine.
I do know what my taste buds say: "I like Uncle Nickie's wine."

A cold winter's day with a visit to some kin to mingle with these friends of mine.
Good food, warmth, conversation and...Uncle Nickie's wine.

The children play together and exhibit traits at which they shine.
While grown ups gather at the kitchen table Uncle Nickie brings out the wine.

A wedge of cheese, black olives sprinkled with red pepper in olive oil so fine.
Home made crusty Italian bread and...Uncle Nickie's wine.

The conversation starts out simple with whatever comes to mind.
Opinions form, with questions asked, as we sip Uncle Nickie's wine.

A piece of bread, a bit of cheese one olive at a time.
A quotation ventured with a pause for a drink of Uncle Nickie's wine.

Afternoon draws into evening, more food consumed
the elders reminiscing now, of the old days they do pine.
The young ones sit and listen...sipping...Uncle Nickie's wine.

As you pass thru life, accumulate memories of your likes and specific finds.
Nothing brings back more pleasant feelings than Uncle Nickie's wine.

The shades of night are drawn now on the making of that wine.
Memories can't be taken away, they grow mellow in the sublime.

It's the ending of an era, just a place in time.
The book of life is closed now, Uncle Nickie has passed down the line.

With careful thought, in retrospect, I've come to realize what created that taste so fine.
It wasn't the grapes or the ingredients...UNCLE NICKIE WAS THE WINE.

John Howard

Uncle Nick passed away this morning at about 5:30 am,
The first day of spring.

March 21, 1999

The Puppy

A hot late summer day, lazy and calm
The kids borrowed my car for a ride to the farm.
A visit with friends, take in the view was the rule.
Check out the animals, pay respects, before returning back to school.

They came back excited with news I should hear.
The dog at the farm had puppies, so dear.
That I should just have one, for my very own good,
Then I wouldn't get lonely, if only I could!

For with four lovely daughters, ranging from the baby of twelve
To the two oldest, of college age.
My life was quite hectic, I couldn't be blue.
I hadn't time to be lonely, restful moments were few.

Being badgered with this pleading of wanting a pup,
The girls were convincing that they would help it grow up.
They would feed it and groom it with all of their heart.
My commitments were nil in giving this puppy its start.

By consenting at last, my arguments lost in the discussion's heat...
They brought home the puppy, cuddled up in the seat.
I happened to notice when we first chanced to meet,
This cute little fellow had some awful big feet.

The girls were quite faithful in their promises to keep.
They cared for the dog for all of a week.
Then mother took over the feeding and care,
For the girls went to school—we picked up their share.

When they came home on school break, they played with the pup.
He was king of the hill as he tried to keep up.
With the playing and petting, the attention galore,
What puppy could want or demand any more?

Puppies are puppies, in this we all will agree.
But puppies grow up to be big dogs, you see.
And grow up he did, in a very short span of time.
He took over the yard, the house, and the chair that was mine.

He acquired quite a figure, such was his pedigree,
A bit of a Husky, Malamute, Shepherd, and others we could see.
As strong of a dog as I'd ever known,
With a temperament to go with it—all of his own.

With children he was gentle, his nature never cross.
But he just kept on growing, like a miniature horse.
He would play just as rough as I wanted to play,
But if I raised a hand to my children, he'd keep me at bay.

If I became overzealous in correcting my brood,
He was sure to remind me to refrain from that mood.
For he would come up behind me, not leaving things to chance…
Then give me a smart nip, in the seat of my pants.

To keep him from wandering, he was chained to a fallen tree.
It must have weighed quite a lot for I couldn't budge it, you see.
I said to myself: "That'll fix you, old boy!"
Next day, he was dragging it around like a toy.
A more permanent fixture was required to retain.
This very large dog with his tethering chain.

After selecting a location, I dug a very deep hole,
Then planted within in, a length of a large telephone pole.

That will hold him, I mumbled, all covered with sweat.
He won't wander now, I was willing to bet.
But next day he was loose, he thought it was a game.
He had twisted and strained, and had broken his chain.

Rivets and chained, 5 hooks and 4 bolts
He wore through them all, it was just, to him, a big joke.
He was trying my patience, testing my will.
This animal wouldn't be broken to ever stay still.

This dog was master of our neighborhood as he was roaming about.
Friendly to the neighbors, who'd notice and give him a handout.
He played with all the children and hardly ever came home,
Answered to no one…he was delighted to roam.

He wouldn't tolerate strangers and would keep them at bay,
Growling and barking till they each went away.
My wife was his keeper, only she he would mind and obey
When I issued a command, he would cock his head as if to say "Not today."

John Howard

The dog was allowed in the house that my wife kept so neat.
He stayed in the breezeway, only after he wiped his feet.
She had trained him to do this; I never knew how it was done.
It was a game that they both played and to him, it was fun.

As he came from outdoors and entered the home,
My wife would acclaim, "Wipe those feet" in just the right tone.
The dog would stop in his tracks, prance in place for a spell,
Walk a set pattern between both doorways till he got the nod
        "all was well."

Then he would settle right down with his own special skill,
Lay in the breezeway with his head on the kitchen doorsill.
This was his place, where with his eyes he could survey,
What went on in the kitchen as he rested that way.

He left us one morning to some area unknown.
A new territory to conquer, a larger space to roam?
Children to meet, to run with, and play,
To give out his magic for a most memorable day.

September 26, 1997

49

A Backward Glance

Yesterday I contemplated my reflection cast out in a stream
Twas like a vision before me brought forth from a dream.

A thin young man with tousled brown hair
Strong, wrinkle-free with skin soft and fair.

The day was his oyster, the world, his pearl.
Climb to the top of the mast and the sail unfurl.

Sally forth into danger; throw care to the wind,
With undaunted spirit to attempt anything.

Today in my bathroom, at the mirror, to shave
I noticed an old man staring back through the haze.

Hair sparse and silver, skin sagging, double chin.
Today was for survival, to exist, not to win.

Blend in with nature, enjoy the beauty, don't tempt fate.
Get closer to your creator before it's too late.

October 21, 1994

Conversation

I have conversed with some very important folks that I've met.
I've hardly said a word, just listened, but yet...
Comments from third parties, which have been overheard
That I'm a great conversationalist,
        Isn't that absurd?

July 1, 1996

Impressions

What is it you see when you look at this face?
Do you judge by the color, the shape, eyes, or race?
Is it the voice that determines my fate?
Does it fit into the character you're trying to shape?

Gaze directly upon this person when you meet,
Don't falter or stare or look down at your feet.
Inspect, converse, find something in common,
Remember that the best part of soup is always at the bottom.

People respond to those who show they care.
Tailor your remarks to observations you both can share.
Be kind in your thoughts, your manners show true.
Whatever you say or do will reflect back on you.

Expound the best virtues of what you observe.
Be a good listener; don't toss out a curve.
Discussing or commenting on what you're all about,
Will only compound and confuse what their mind is sorting out.

Don't correct or condemn and never complain,
For it will only come back as coarse comments and shame.
Stand up straight, be honest, endure the pain.
If you've caused a problem, speak up, take the blame.

Be attentive to the speaker, that's what conversation's about.
Enter comments or thoughts when asked, but don't shout.
If you ask pertinent questions that are reflections of what you observe,
The topic is first person; you'll be remembered as you deserve.

This only goes to show what ego is all about.
We only remember the good points when it's time to cull it out.
Let someone make a comment that goes against the grain,
Then that's when you'll find the thunder, the lightening and rain.

It's best to keep the mouth shut when you have nothing nice to say.
For it will only foster hate and discontent for you to carry on your
        way.
There is nothing like ill feelings to make a person sad.
It is better to search for a good point than to dwell upon the bad.

All these comments are small lessons that I have learned throughout
        my life.
Some were born through good times, while others times of strife.
Try your best to keep in mind all the good points I have made.
Then you'll never have to worry about making the best grade.

October 1, 1997

Autumn in New England

The temperature is dropping, the feeling of frost in the air.
Look about in wonder at nature's pallet to stare.
For now the trees have stopped nourishment to all of their leaves.
Jack Frost has started coloring the bushes and trees.

In the swamps, the maples lead the show,
With splotches of vermilion and bright yellow as they glow.
A challenge to others to join the blossoming landscape.
Each day it enhances with color the picture to shape.

The birch, the nut trees spread upward on the side of the hill,
Throw out yellow splashes to give nature's canvas its thrill.
Our eyes gently travel to the valley and below.
We notice gray shadows, green trees not yet caught up in the show.

The oak and sugar maple now give off their flair,
Flaming red and burnt orange to the canvas they share.
Each day we gaze out in wonder as the convergence of color takes place.
The peak of the season is upon us as we drink in the splendor that we face.

Vivid colors, white houses, green pasture...
        Church steeples, soft clouds on blue sky,
New England's landscape in Autumn—
        Quite pleasant to the eye.
A crisp frosty morning as we brace for our walk
Smoke gently rising from the chimneys, breath fogging the air, quiet...
        And peaceful—no need to talk.

I stare out, in awe, at the splendor of this beautiful site.
It's that time of the year, once more, a true Painter's delight.

October 6, 1997

The Captain

He sits on the porch in his old rocking chair
Watching the sun going down, taking in the night air.
Overlooking the mountains, blue ridges on high.
Towering formations reaching out to the sky.

Red sun behind the hills, giving off a bright glare,
Bouncing off puffy white clouds as we stare.
Watching in awe as they billow over the peaks,
Sunbeams between them in shimmering streaks.

The battle is in earnest just over that rise.
With fire in the sky, it appears to our eyes.
The Captain will come visiting when this engagement is done.
We will just have to wait till the setting of the sun.

The mist in the dell is beginning to rise,
Weird shapes are now forming as we visualize.
Cavalry drilling on the meadow below,
It is the Captain's own company forming up for the show.

The breeze is increasing up high on the hill.
Bunching the clouds together with never ending skill.
Thunder is the sound rumbling in the distance away.
Must be the artillery playing their song in this fray.

The Captain was killed in battle in 1864.
His body is buried in the soft earth of this valley floor.
Life given up in a long drawn out cause,
His spirit wanders about, still fighting his war.

John Howard

He visits quite often on these hot summer nights.
When the air is still, in the pale moonlight.
There is no sound to make his presence known.
It is a feeling you experience when you're rocking—all alone.

It's just imagination, or so people say.
Your knowledge of history and his spirit won't make him go away.
He just keeps me company when his duties are done.
We sit quietly together rocking as one.

Now it is peaceful, it's quiet, a smell of rain in the air.
Lightening flashes in the mountains, the battle's raging out there.
Sound of thunder getting closer, the breeze picking up to a blow.
It won't be long now before the Captain has to go.

The first drops of rain start to spatter the ground.
I look for the Captain but he is now not around.
The spell has been broken, the sound of a train coming thru.
Time to go on inside, I've given the Captain his due.

October 6, 2000

Winter Is On Its Way

The wind is gusting off the mountain,
The flag straight out in the fray.
Sunlight warm against your face but…
Winter is on its way.

The trees have dropped their colorful leaves,
The mountain is casting shades of brown and gray.
Crisp air, blue sky, no haze in the valley, but…
Winter is on its way.

The temperature is still warm, no need for heavy clothes
To ward off the cold this day.
A little crispness in the breeze ~ warning…
Winter is on its way.

The Coal Train slowly climbing on its struggle over the mountain
        pass.
The echo of the engine, churning as it labors so far away.
The whistle sounding mournfully, ever distant…
Winter is on its way.

Eagles spread on lofty winds now appear o're the mountain top.
Soaring higher on thermals, majestically flying south this day.
Another harbinger of things to come…
Winter is on its way.

John Howard

Cornstalks have dried out now, pumpkins in abundance,
Halloween critters held at bay.
Jack Frost showed early this morning...
Winter is on its way.

Summer has surely left us,
Or so the old folks say.
'Twas a season to remember now that...
Winter is on its way.

The Sand Pile

It's a place that children are drawn to
Like a bee to a flower pod.
That inconspicuous little hill...
The sand pile in my yard.

It appeared there quite accidentally,
Leftover sand from the construction trade,
Slowly growing after many jobs,
A little hill was made.

I knew that I would have a use for it.
Eventually a job would come along,
Requiring sand for fill or concrete work.
It wouldn't stay there long.

The children soon claimed that pile as theirs;
Toy trucks, planes, little shovels, doll clothes,
Always picking up remnants of day's activity.
What they played at - Heaven knows!

Children from round the neighborhood
Congregated at that pile of sand.
Played King of the Hill, made castles,
served up mud pies, made by hand.

The mothers knew where the kids had played
When they came home from my yard.
With their dirty hands and dirty feet,
Sand packed in their hair quite hard.

John Howard

The rings around the bathtub told tales
Of where that child had been.
Even though the kids played out of sight
Their appearance spelled out the scene.

The laughter, the songs, the merriment
Happy children in their time
The fun, the games, the dirt and the grime
On that big pile of sand of mine

As the children worked that sand pile down
I replenished it each time
A new load of sand would reappear
the kids would revel in its find

My children are all grown up now
the sand pile is still waiting for their attack
My grandchildren now play upon that pile
when their mothers turn their back

Old toys stored under the back stairs
waiting for the children to appear
that old sand pile is waiting
for the next generation to come near.

To My Children

I may not have given credit, when credit was surely due.
For praise must be earned, or it won't mean much to you.

Of this I have been lax, I know this, be assured.
Forgive me this sin, for I'd like to be cured.

To give praise when it is needed,
To take note of deeds when good deeds are done,
To be truthful and honest and above all... sincere,
Not to make bad jokes, or laugh, or poke fun.

If an apology is needed, please accept this as such.
For I don't mean to hurt you... I love you too much.

August 14, 1994

John Howard

The Funnel of Life

Boldly forward we race, holding our banners high
as we dash about, ever forward in our pursuit
searching for that elusive pie up in the sky
that we call our goal in life. To reach for
that plateau that is always evasive
and just beyond our grasp. Is
that our quest? Is that what's
best? This struggle to attain
what we desire only to
discover when we get
there that the
sacrifice, the
toll of life,
casting
away,
what
was
held
dear,
turns
out to
be a
n
o
t
h
i
n
g

Sept. 1, 1994

The Old Carpenter's Hammer

I hate to put it away, that hammer of mine.
It fits me like a glove, hammers true and in line.
We've been together thru good times and bad.
It's hard to give it up, it makes me feel sad.

I hold it and feel it as I reminisce back -
Of the places I've been and how it got packed,
to come along for the work I had planned to get done,
for the making of money or just building for fun.

It has been used in the wrecking of old buildings and such
Along with the creation of a new house as much.
It has pried out the nails from the back of a stair
As well as pulling tight the rungs of an old kitchen chair.

It is held in a sheath fastened tight to my belt.
I would be lost on the job without all of its help.
In ripping and banging, driving a nail,
It is there when I need it, never to fail.

Amazing as it seems, it has performed many feats;
Like prying and twisting, aligning wood sheets,
As we build and create many things out of wood.
It has various uses... but that's understood.

Like removing the cap on a bottle of beer,
Or driving a wedge to level out a pier.

It has worn very well and brought me no shame.
Of its care I've been lax, even left it out in the rain.

Packed it in a box with other tools in my truck.
Used it to dig out a pipe in the ground that was stuck.

Beat out some tin to flash in a brick.
Use the claw end of the hammer to sharpen a stick.

Break up some wood to stake out for a walk,
Fill a crack up with oakum and drive in the caulk.

It should be gold plated or placed in a shrine,
That's the least I should do for that old buddy of mine.
For it's made me good money - held me in esteem for my work,
Been strong and unyielding in my demands, with no shirk.

In ways that I used it... not intended as such,
But it still out-performed many tools just as much.
So I'll hang you up gently on my workbench, you see,
That way when I'm puttering, you'll always be there for me.

Summer Day at Lake Combie

Small fish hovering gently as they swim
          below this dock,
Ever mindless of their movement,
          not affected by the clock.

I sit here just day-dreaming on this
          hot and breathless day,
A soft breeze caresses me as it passes
          along its way.

Across the placid water, making concentric
          unfolding ripples, dancing to the fray.
As it proceeds ever constant across this
          serene and secluded bay.

The soft brown doe blends into the foliage
          as it slowly walks on down the hill.
Falling in behind is a speckled fawn
          staying close to the mother's will.

Both bending at the water's edge to drink
          from this pleasant lake
The cool refreshing nourishment of which
          they both partake.

A movement of the hillside grass now
          activates my eye.
The jackrabbit bounding noiselessly,
          searching for a tender morsel to try.

John Howard

Two red-headed woodpeckers now appear, their
          red heads bending to and fro.
Listening to something that I cannot hear...
          before they decide to go.

A squirrel bounds from branch to branch
          seeking nuts with his practical eye.
In this giant tree with spreading limbs
          reaching out toward the sky.

Some partridge now appear moving quickly
          down the hillside, all marching in a row.
The mother hen leads her scurrying
          brood of 12 chicks all in tow.

The peacefulness and serenity overwhelms me
          in this spectacular grand showcase.
The Lord has blessed me and filled my cup
          with the beauty of this place.

Auburn, California
July 16, 2003

Reflections II

Take a moment here to just reflect
To suspend yourself in time of retrospect
Look back in your past to what you have seen
Think of things you have touched and where you have been

To appreciate those brilliant warm sunbeams
That wake up the senses and create pleasant dreams
Here are a few thoughts to start it all going
To kick up the process and get the juice flowing

A walk thru a forest on a moss covered trail
A drink of cold spring water from an old oak pail

A sip of iced lemonade on a hot summer's day
The smell in the morning of newly mowed hay

The touch of a baby's hand as it explores your face
The feeling of family at the table saying grace

The moon over the ocean on a warm summer's night
Ice crystals on the window pane in the cold morning light

Savor these thoughts as you read over each line
Alert all your senses as you look back in time
Create a feeling from deeply within
Those hidden recesses to relive it again

What a wonderful feeling to brighten up your day
To bring back fond memories that have been tucked away.

John Howard

A View From the Window

This is a place that I reside at on this fine late autumn day.
Placed high on a well manicured hillside, overlooking a bay.

Billowy white clouds drifting lazily, in a blue sky, on their way
To wherever they are going on this bright sunlit day.

The flag is blowing briskly in the wind, on the flagpole in the yard.
White swans feeding among the jagged rocks, forever on their guard.

A lone seagull flying gracefully, as he circles over the bay,
Ever watchful of the water, just looking for some prey.

Boats all wrapped for winter, stored safe upon the land.
The boatyard across the bay is desolate, no one is at hand.

The setting sun upon the horizon reflects bright lights within the
    clouds,
Shades of red, blue, orange, and gold in the sky do so abound.
this is a scene from the Lord's pallet, a view that truly astounds.

Apple Rehab, Watch Hill, RI
December 7, 2011

The Promise of Spring

The crocus are blooming and the tulips are rising
        in the gardens along the roadway
There is movement in the boatyard where the boats
        are stored and all wrapped up on this day
Take note of this activity... for spring is on its way.

The sun is getting warmer in the
        beginning of this day
With the grass growing ever greener in
        the fields above the bay

The daffodils are exposing yellow blossoms
        along the roadsides
Tulips pushing out their leaves with buds
        showing other flowers far and wide

Bluebells bright with color accent the
        arrangements about the flower beds
Foretelling promises of what
        the winter snows have shed

The brightness of the sun on this
        clear and cloudless day
Masks the cool temperature as the wind
        blows over the bay

Wintertime is over
          or so it must seem
But this is springtime in New England
          weather changes quickly to interrupt our dreams

So take whatever is provided in this
          ever changing scene
Accept that which is given on this cool
          and windy day
Bask in the sun and enjoy it as springtime
          winds along its way

Ralphina

To slowly stroll near the water of the ever rolling sea
Hand in hand, barely touching, it's just you and me.

A balmy breeze blowing, gently caressing o're my face
Like the wisp of the touch of some loose woven silk lace.

Your touch and the warmth of your hand clasped in mine
Makes my heart start to flutter, swell up with a feeling quite fine.

Romantic music in the distance catches our ear from afar
The sound rising and falling, chords light from a guitar.

The smell of your perfume, your scent thrills me thru and thru
A feeling of elation just to be here with you.

The heightening of the senses, like a taste of good wine
Just having you near and knowing you're mine.

You have been here beside me for many a year
It's comforting knowing that you're always quite near.

You're my essence, my being, the light of my life
My lover, my best friend, but mostly, my wife.

John Howard

A Rainy Spring Day

This dreary, rainy, windy day
Expresses feelings of depression or dismay

The birds are not present in their foraging for food
They are seeking shelter from this cold and gloomy mood

Contractors, carpenters and landscapers -
        not working on the estates or the grounds
The ocean is restless, large swells do so abound

A good book held within my hands
        soft music filling the room so fair
A coffee mug resting on the table next to me
        within reach of my easy chair

I feel for the fisherman on the water this day
For the small draggers and lobster boats out for their prey

The swells and windy waves causing the small boats to rock
Makes me marvel that they should ever have left the safety of the dock

I sit at my window, I wonder and day dream
As I take in the view of this ever changing scene

It never ceases to amaze me of nature's constant change
The ever changing scenery of my limited range

The 4th of July

Rise out of bed this summer morn
To celebrate this day that freedom was born.
Anticipate the joy of things to come
The holiday spirit dictates what will be done.

Patriotic parade through the village street
Flags unfurled, banners flowing, children marching to the
      drummer's beat
Vehicles decked out in red, blue, and white
A joy to behold in the bright sunlight.

We all congregate at the village green
Relatives, neighbors and visitors, all to be seen
Small talk, hearty greetings to friends from far away
This once a year gathering is a highlight of the day

John Howard

The Administrator

She stands upon the open porch,
        her hands resting upon the rail
A warm breeze is blowing gently,
        watching boats, traversing the river, under sail.

Her mind is far away
        as her eyes take in this scenic bay
For her job encompasses many facets
        that she must attend to on this pleasant day.

This is just a break to enjoy the breeze
        as it caresses her silken blond hair
A moment to contemplate, to make a decision,
        as she overlooks her domain, her lair.

This facility that she manages
        sits proudly upon a gentle hill
Overlooking a bay and boatyard
        with residents requiring care and special skill.

She navigates through this residence listening
        to the gripes, complaints, special needs and care
While balancing budgets, maintenance, health issues
        with a smile and understanding nature that she is aware.

She may not be able to fix everything
        but she will damn well try
For this is her home and quest
        the apple of her eye.

Apple Rehab
August 12, 2012

The Traveler

She is well up into her 90's,
      confined to bed and her private wheelchair.
Some days she is really quite with it
      while other days she is not at all aware.
Some days are extremely comfortable for her,
      while others fall into despair.

Still she travels about in her wheelchair
      wheeling and pulling, in her workout, to get anywhere.
She is not about to give it up,
      the manipulating of that chair.

Old age has taken her hearing
      with her focus limited to one eye.
She is just a wrinkled elderly woman
      with the world just passing her by.

I often had coffee in the morning, with this woman
      who was always sweet, vivacious, and gay,
But time has not been kind to this person
      and has taken these qualities away.

Now she does not recognize me,
      as we pass each other in the hall.
She will either ignore me and not speak to me
      or cuss me out like a drunken sailor in a brawl

But I will always have the memories
      of how she was in days now past
As she blocks your passage in the hallways
      she has got your notice - at last.

Reflections

I sit upon my easy chair,
        my eyes are slowly closing.
The book is open upon my lap,
        my mind is ever dozing.

For it is time to reminisce now, to bring back...
        times of things and places long past
The technicolor from the back of my mind
        to revisit old thoughts, at last.

To remember the white sand, balmy breezes, palm trees,
        the sound of soft music or steel drums fill the air.
The exotic paradise is forming on my mind
        throwing pictures on my eyelids - oh! so fair.

To recall these special memories of pleasant moments
        all rolled up in my past
Can be called back again, played over and over
        for my enjoyment while they last.

A walk in time is what they call this
        the memory is vivid, I can say that it never dulls.
But as I grow deeper into my pleasant reflections,
        I am back there, reminiscing, with all the thrills.

It cheers me up, this lifeline place of where I'm at
      within my mind and vision
Depression and distress have vanished from my thoughts
      like having been released from my prison

If only I could walk back in time
      to relive these thoughts of mine
I wouldn't change a single image
      of these beautiful thoughts... and how they shine.

October 1, 2012

September Observations

White contrails from an aircraft
flying oh so high.
     Streaks of puffy white clouds
     drifting thru the clear blue sky

A crystal crisp morning
no breeze upon the air
     With promises of sunshine
     make up this day so fair

In the bay, a group of ducks
paddling effortlessly, so it seems
     Paints a picture of serenity
     that conjures up dreams

Of something so pleasant,
a vision to the eye
     Catch the setting, for remembering
     don't let it pass you by

The whisper of the wind now caresses
the under branches of the trees
     Quietly moving the leaves
     as they sway upon the breeze

The rays of the sun warm the air
pushing up from the south
     Paints a very pleasant picture
     that you can save for yourself

Watch the egret standing
in the low water, among the reeds
    Sifting the shoreline for tiny
    plankton for to feed

Check the high flying osprey
searching the sky for its prey
    Watching Mother Nature ever
    evolving on this day

This is a wonder to behold, this always changing scene
you only have to be observant, place your mind at ease
    To float on thru the day, pay attention is what I mean
    The observations are quite clear now...
    Preserve them for a cold mid-winter dream.

October 20, 2012

Northeast Storm

Storm clouds racing across the sky
Forecasting tales of days gone by
The wind whipping waves on the rocks in the bay
As this Nor'easter travels swiftly on its way

Raindrops spattered on the window panes
outlines this picture of which it frames
No sun shining thru these gray clouds
the boatyard is silent - no work or sounds

A lone gull hovering over the windswept bay
battling the wind as its wings shift fighting its way
Heading inland in search of some stable air
To hunt for food or feel safe in its lair

We sit at the window on this dreary fall day
Watching the waves whip up in the bay
Observing the scene in our own special way
Looking for sunlight to cheer up our stay

The wind is now buffeting against the window pane
Making trails with new formations from the driving rain
There is a trace of blue showing in the eastern sky
Bringing special pleasant thoughts to the watching eye

John Howard

Hope springs up in its marvelous way
Giving happy signs of the warmth of a sunny day
There are signals in the distance of what will come
Tomorrow will be pleasant with lots of sun

My eyes behold what we have had to face
The aftermath of Mother Nature's haste
To wreak havoc upon this special place
Be thankful of sparing us from harm with God's Grace.

November 8, 2012
Northeastern Storm after Super Storm Sandy

A Moment in Time

Come travel with me on this cold winter's day
As I sit in my easy chair and watch time while away

We dream of warm weather, soft breezes, tropic air
Close your eyes and imagine yourself being there

The tropics now beckon with soft sand in your toes
Warm water covers your footsteps with its soft moving flows

The warm sun on your body as you walk on this shore
Makes you feel as being at peace with yourself ever more

Just sitting here day-dreaming and biding my time
With a feeling of contentment ever so fine

Pelicans are diving for fish, I observe, out to sea
Dolphins chasing the bait fish ever closer to me

The water shimmering silver as the bait rise from below
Mother Nature at her finest puts on quite a show

I have witnessed these offerings as I have traveled thru time
My memories remain fresh as I recall them from my mind

It is great to just sit here and look back into time
To recall pleasant feelings and to say 'they are all mine'

January 2, 2013

Made in the USA
Charleston, SC
04 February 2014